Mount Rushmore

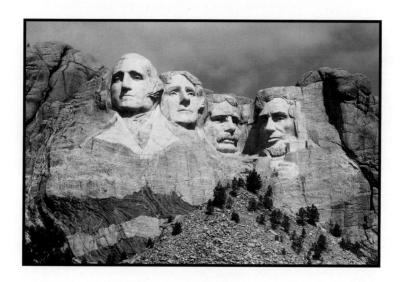

by Susan Ashley

Reading consultant: Susan Nations, M.Ed., author/literacy coach/consultant

WEEKLY WR READER®
EARLY LEARNING LIBRARY

Please visit our web site at: www.earlyliteracy.cc
For a free color catalog describing Weekly Reader® Early Learning Library's
list of high-quality books, call 1-877-445-5824 (USA) or 1-800-387-3178 (Canada).
Weekly Reader® Early Learning Library's fax: (414) 336-0164.

Library of Congress Cataloging-in-Publication Data

Ashley, Susan.
    Mount Rushmore / by Susan Ashley.
      p. cm. — (Places in American history)
    Includes bibliographical references and index.
    Summary: An introduction to the history and creation of South Dakota's Mount Rushmore
National Memorial, where the images of four presidents are sculpted into the mountain.
    ISBN 0-8368-4142-5 (lib. bdg.)
    ISBN 0-8368-4149-2 (softcover)
    1. Mount Rushmore National Memorial (S.D.)—Juvenile literature. [1. Mount Rushmore
National Memorial (S.D.) 2. National monuments.] I. Title. II. Series.
    F657.R8A84 2004
    978.3'93—dc22
                                                 2003062104

This edition first published in 2004 by
Weekly Reader® Early Learning Library
330 West Olive Street, Suite 100
Milwaukee, WI 53212 USA

Editor: JoAnn Early Macken
Art direction, cover and layout design: Tammy Gruenewald
Photo research: Diane Laska-Swanke

Photo credits: Cover, title, pp. 7, 20 © James P. Rowan; p. 4 © Gibson Stock Photography;
p. 5 Kami Koenig/© Weekly Reader Early Learning Library, 2004; pp. 6, 14 Rise Studio;
pp. 8, 9, 11 © Stock Montage, Inc.; p. 10 Charles D'Emery; p. 12 Victor Fintak; pp. 13, 18
Lincoln Borglum; p. 15 Joe W. McCully; pp. 16, 17 Bell Photo; p. 21 National Park Service

Printed in the United States of America

1 2 3 4 5 6 7 8 9 08 07 06 05 04

Table of Contents

Mount Rushmore towers above the Black Hills.

On the Side of a Mountain

Mount Rushmore is one of the largest monuments in the United States. It is a huge outdoor sculpture. The faces of four U.S. presidents are carved on the side of a mountain.

The faces of Presidents George Washington, Thomas Jefferson, Theodore Roosevelt, and Abraham Lincoln are carved on the mountain. The faces look out over the Black Hills in western South Dakota.

Mount Rushmore is in western South Dakota.

Mount Rushmore was carved
on a large granite cliff.

A Monument for South Dakota

The idea for the monument began in the 1920s.
People in South Dakota were thinking of ways to
bring visitors to their state. A man named Doane
Robinson wanted to create a big monument. He
hoped that would bring people to South Dakota.

Robinson hired Gutzon Borglum to carve the monument. Borglum was an artist. He liked to make large sculptures. He had carved a huge figure on the side of a mountain in Georgia.

Gutzon Borglum carved the side of Stone Mountain in Georgia.

Robinson had a plan for the monument. He wanted it to honor heroes of the American West. Borglum had a different idea. He wanted to carve national heroes. He chose four popular U.S. presidents.

Gutzon Borglum designed Mount Rushmore.

George Washington was
the nation's first president.
Thomas Jefferson helped
the nation grow. Abraham
Lincoln held the nation
together during the Civil
War. He also freed the
slaves. Theodore
Roosevelt kept the nation
strong. He also loved the
West. He created many
national parks there.

George Washington was
the first president of the
United States.

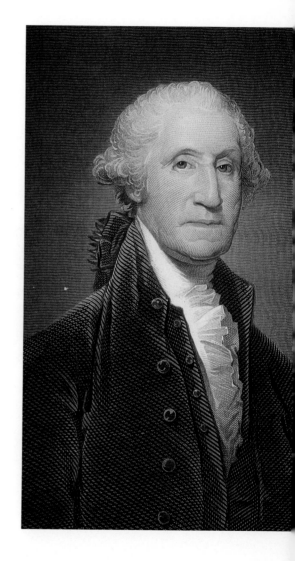

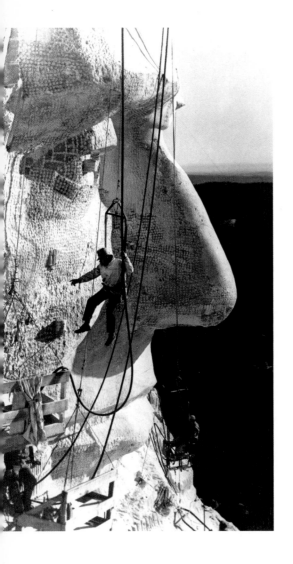

Carving a Mountain

Carving Mount Rushmore would not be easy. Borglum had to find the right men for the job. Some of the men he hired were miners. The miners knew how to work with rock. This job was like nothing they had ever done before.

The men on Mount Rushmore had to work high above the ground.

The miners were used to working underground. To build the monument, they worked high in the air. They climbed hundreds of steps to get to work each day. Then they sat in swings that hung over the side of the mountain.

Workers hung in midair as they carved George Washington's face.

Dynamite blasted away
large pieces of rock.

The men used dynamite to blast away huge
chunks of rock. They had to be careful. Dynamite
is dangerous. They also had to be sure not to
blast away too much rock.

The men carved the faces with hammers and chisels. They worked while they dangled hundreds of feet in the air. It was hard work, but they were proud to be carving Mount Rushmore.

Workers used different tools to carve the faces.

It took many years to carve the faces
on Mount Rushmore.

Washington's face was the first to be carved.
Jefferson's face was second. Lincoln's was third,
and Roosevelt's was the last. It took fourteen
years to finish the faces. Borglum had wanted
to carve the men down to their waists. There
was not enough time or money.

Other problems came up, too. Jefferson was supposed to be on the other side of Washington. The rock there was too soft. Roosevelt is set farther back than the others. Bad rock had to be removed from that area.

Workers first carved Thomas Jefferson to the left of George Washington.

ELEVATION
ONE MILE ABOVE
SEA LEVEL

VIEW
MONUMENT
FROM STUDIO
300 FEET
GOOD TRAIL
INFORMATION

Each time a face was complete, a ceremony was held. Several presidents came to the Black Hills to make speeches. People came to see Mount Rushmore even before it was finished. They had never seen anything like it.

President Franklin Delano Roosevelt visited Mount Rushmore in 1936.

In 1941, Gutzon Borglum died. His son Lincoln took over the project. Later that year, work on Mount Rushmore stopped for good. The United States entered World War II.

Lincoln Borglum finished Mount Rushmore after his father died.

The faces on Mount Rushmore are huge!

Visiting Mount Rushmore

People who visit Mount Rushmore can see how big the faces are. Each head is as tall as a five-story building. Each nose is twice as high as a classroom ceiling.

Mount Rushmore Facts

Mount Rushmore is 5,725 feet
  (1,745 meters) high.

Each face is 60 feet (18 m) high.

Each nose is 20 feet (6 m) long.

Each eye is 11 feet (3.4 m) wide.

Each mouth is 18 feet (5.5 m) wide.

If their entire bodies were carved, each
  president would be 465 feet (142 m) tall.

Mount Rushmore is a popular place to visit.

Millions of people visit Mount Rushmore each
year. They can stop at a museum. They can visit
an information center. They can look at Gutzon
Borglum's studio. They can even see the tools
that were used to carve the mountain.

Mount Rushmore honors four presidents who had great hopes for their country. It is also a monument to the people who built it. They worked hard to create something that would inspire people for years to come.

Mount Rushmore honors four U.S. presidents.

Glossary

carve — to make a shape by cutting into a hard material

ceremony — a formal celebration

chisels — tools used to cut rocks

dynamite — an explosive used to blast away rock

honor — to show respect

inspire — to make someone think or feel deeply about something

miners — people who work in a mine

monument — a sculpture or building made to honor important people or events

sculpture — a statue or form often made of stone, metal, or wood

studio — the place where an artist works

For More Information

Books

Gabriel, Luke S. *Mount Rushmore: From Mountain to Monument*. Chanhassen, Minn.: The Child's World, 2000.

Rau, Dana Meachen. *Mount Rushmore*. Minneapolis: Compass Point Books, 2002.

Santella, Andrew. *Mount Rushmore*. Danbury, Conn.: Children's Press, 1999.

Web Sites

American Experience: Mount Rushmore
www.pbs.org/wgbh/amex/rushmore
Timeline, photos, and information about carving the monument

Mount Rushmore National Monument
www.serve.com/wizjd/pics/rush01_m.jpg
Large photo of Mount Rushmore

Travel South Dakota: Mount Rushmore
www.travelsd.com/parks/rushmore/
Information about visiting Mount Rushmore

Index

About the Author

Susan Ashley has written over eighteen books for children, including two picture books about dogs, *Puppy Love* and *When I'm Happy, I Smile.* She enjoys animals and writing about them. Susan lives in Wisconsin with her husband and two frisky felines.